## THE HEALING POWER OF LOVE

Recommended by many psychiatrists and psychologists as bibliotherapy, HEARTS THAT WE BROKE LONG AGO speaks to us about loving, and also about how our past, with all its old wounds, influences our present.

We are all pilgrims in search of happiness and love. Yet why, when love is offered, do we time and time again find ourselves lost and confused? In HEARTS THAT WE BROKE LONG AGO Merle Shain shows us how we unknowingly become the killers of our own best dreams. Wise, tender, filled with insights, her book touches our innermost feelings and brings them into focus with sudden clarity.

### HEARTS THAT WE BROKE
### LONG AGO
*Merle Shain's books are like good poetry:*
*They put words to feelings for which*
*there were no words before.*

*Books by Merle Shain*

SOME MEN ARE MORE PERFECT THAN OTHERS

WHEN LOVERS ARE FRIENDS

HEARTS THAT WE BROKE LONG AGO

*Merle Shain*

# HEARTS THAT WE BROKE LONG AGO

*Bantam Books*

*Toronto • New York • London • Sydney • Auckland*

HEARTS THAT WE BROKE LONG AGO
*A Bantam Book*

PRINTING HISTORY
McClelland & Stewart edition / September 1983
Seal Trade edition / March 1985
Bantam Hardcover edition / September 1983
Bantam Trade edition / March 1985

Library of Congress Cataloging in Publication Data
Shain, Merle.
    Hearts that we broke long ago.
    1. Conduct of life.  2. Emotions.  3. Interpersonal
relations.  4. Success.  5. Mental health.  I. Title.
BF637.C5S5  1983      158'.24      83-90650
ISBN 0-553-34125-1 (pbk.)

PRINTED IN THE UNITED STATES OF AMERICA
S      0 9 8 7 6 5 4 3 2 1

For my son
—should he ever wonder
if I loved him enough

And my father
who I never got to
tell how much I did.

# Contents

PART ONE     — THE WOUND AND THE
                  KNIFE                            1

             1   — *How tender is the human heart*    3
             2   — *What I did for love or*
                       *A likely story*                 10
             3   — *Take what you want, said God,*
                       *and pay for it*                  18

PART TWO     — SELF-AFFIRMATION     25

             4   — *No one ever loved anyone like*
                       *anyone wants to be loved*      27
             5   — *The wild arrows of pain*        36
             6   — *It doesn't matter if you are*
                       *chained by a golden chain or*
                       *an iron one*                   46

PART THREE     — SELF-HEALING     57

    7   — *Unwind the solemn twine*     59

    8   — *It is better to light candles than*
         *to curse the darkness*     69

    9   — *Compassion is the thing that*
         *leads you gently back to yourself*    77


PART FOUR     — GRACE     85

   10   — *Love is more thicker than forget /*
         *more thinner than recall*     87

   11   — *The brightest star in the darkest*
         *night*     97

   12   — *Don't be alone too long*     110

The nightingales are sobbing in
The orchards of our mothers,
And hearts that we broke long ago
Have long been breaking others;

—"Master and Boatswain"
from *Collected Poems of W. H. Auden*

# HEARTS
# THAT WE
# BROKE
# LONG AGO

*Part One*

# THE WOUND AND THE KNIFE

# 1

## *How tender is the human heart*

I knew a girl once who was involved in an impossible love affair. Impossible because it appeared to be, at least to those of us watching, unrequited.

There is a spell cast by persons sometimes, although cast by whom I only suspect, which when in effect snares its victim in unconscious drives and fragmenting forces—and this girl was certainly under such a spell.

This man she cared about rarely called her, but she called him. He put her on hold. She called back. He gave back her presents. She bought him more. He gave parties but invited others and not her.

Once they were to go on a trip together, and when she arrived, he failed to answer his bell. When in terror she got the superintendent to let her in, he said disdainfully that, as she was three minutes late, she would have to wait in the car. Which she did for close to an hour before he deigned to make an appearance and several hours more until he allowed himself to be entertained.

This man had a wife from whom he had been separated for nine or more years but whom he didn't want to hurt, or so he said, so he and the girl who loved him could not go anywhere anyone might see them. But the girl accepted that and made them little dinners at her place for which he often failed to show. And sometimes, afterwards, she heard where and with whom he'd been, but she always forgave him and asked him to dinner again.

It was painful to watch this love affair. And love affair is what I have to call it because it was clear she'd given this man her whole heart, even though all she seemed to be getting back for her efforts was disappointment and rejection.

And there were days when I tired of her stories of his latest offense and her endless analysis of how his mother had failed him and demanded that she ask herself what it was she got from this. And there were days when I would have liked to ask her why it was she wanted it, and why, if she wished to drown herself, she was torturing herself with shallow water.

But I never asked her, never even spoke the words, because as I looked at her sitting there so prettily telling me yet another of the lies she was telling to herself, I could not see her anymore—I could only see myself.

I would start at the beginning if I knew where the beginning was, but I do not know for sure. I only suspect that it all starts with the first deep wound, and after that, like a person who limps or cradles their withered arm close to their side, we favor the place where the knife went in.

Each of us carries with us an inner knowledge about the way we have been and will be betrayed; so there are those who believe we make it happen out of our unrest. But maybe it is simply that great needs cause great fears, and great fears keep us needful long into the night. I do not know the answers, I only know it happens far more than one would wish and that many people remain pilgrims and never come to peace.

Perhaps it is that the first big hurt is like a Trojan horse deep within the person injured, emitting tiny poisons in the form of fears, so that after that we opt for the pulsation of perhaps rather than trust in what might be just another emotional trompe d'oeil.

Or maybe it's that the frisson which we associate with love is that shudder we experienced as a child, so if we once loved someone who rejected us, or slipped the rug out one day, when we choose to experience love again we seek out the same old thrill, someone who will do with us that minuet we once did.

I only know that in time many of us list to starboard, our needs growing greater but unmet, and whenever the gods conspire to give us a chance to make ourselves whole, we close the doors fast because the needs which are threatened are too great.

There is an old Hindu saying about the melon and the knife: "Whether the melon falls on the knife or the knife falls on the melon," the saying goes, "it's the melon that suffers." And so it would appear to me.

Some of us hurl ourselves at life, and others crouch and wait for it to roll up over us, but you can usually tell who it is who is taking on life and who it is who is fending it off and whether this is a new game or whether it is old.

The girl who reminded me of myself and I, we've been through the wars, or maybe, as the Buddhists say, we've just been doing it again until we got it right.

I could tell you many stories of how we are our own worst friends. Of men as well as women because no one is immune. I could tell you the story of a man I know whose family fled from Europe when he was just a boy and how he grew up a stranger in another land. And how he struggled to renounce the part of him that was foreign now, and to adopt the ways that were thought well of in the place where he now was. And what it cost him then, and costs him still, and how he still tries to pass, but in doing so has lost himself.

Or I could tell you of another friend, one whose parents had divorced when he was small, and how his mother's anger at his father and her stories of how he'd done her wrong made him hate his father and therefore hate himself. And I could tell you about the years it took him to find out who he was. And all the pain he caused himself because he didn't want to know.

Or I could tell you more about my friend, the one who reminded me of myself, because like the cat who is said to return to the place where it once lived, she went home and home again. The first person she ever loved was her father whom she could never please, and this man she was trying so hard to win, the one with the iron band locked around his heart, was just a substitute for him, someone with whom she could play at trying to please her father still.

But it would be wrong to suggest that life is simple, or that there is a cause for every effect, so I will simply say, as Oscar Wilde once did, "When the gods wish to punish us, they answer our prayers." Which means of course that it is often very difficult to tell the wound from the knife.

There are few men who dare to publish to the world the prayers they make to Almighty God, but I will do so now. If I had one wish, I'd wish my father stayed longer in this world. Long enough at least for him to spread his joy and me to spread my wings.

I cannot help but wonder how my life would have been different if my father had not died when I was twelve. Whether I would have grown up to be a different person than the one that I am now. One as often the garden as the gardener. One who did not always have to be brave.

It has been said that a lot of women of our generation "grew up to be the men they always wanted to marry," and that is true of me, but would it have been so had my father lived? Who is there to say?

But there are no answers to those questions, and I will never know what I would have been like had I not had liberation thrust upon me at an early age, or even whether I would have liked me if I'd have met me with the heart that I have now.

I am part of all that I have met, and so, my friend,

are you, and most of us would have skipped a chapter here and there if we were the ones to choose. But in the end it doesn't matter how what happened to you made you what you are today, only if you want to be there, and if it feeds you enough for you to stay.

"April is the cruelest month," T.S. Eliot said, because it involves rebirth, and most of us would rather lie dormant yet and not quite come to life. But just as we have to walk with love we have to walk toward fear, and we must know what hurts a lot and look it in the teeth.

"I have to figure out why he's doing it," the friend who reminded me of myself said to me one day. "I suppose you could if you tried long and hard enough," I answered her, "but there is a better question, one that I am trying to ask myself. You could ask yourself why you are doing it, and put your energy into that."

They are singing songs of love, but not for me, you say. But why not, I ask, and you must too. "The girl who can't dance says the band can't play" is what a Yiddish proverb hints, and that's what I suspect. The older I get, the clearer it becomes to me that no one is cheated in this world, unless it's by himself.

## 2

# *What I did for love*
## *or*
# *A likely story*

There was a man once who spent his infancy with his grandmother because his mother followed his father to a foreign posting, leaving him in what she understood to be good hands. The mother, large with second child, returned when he was three, and from then on he lived with his parents. But he never got over his mother's rejection, never got over his dislike for his new brother. And he spent his lifetime auditioning for her approval and for that of those who took her place. And he never stopped competing with anyone he feared was gaining on him, although he outdistanced most of them in the first or second lap.

Fueled by this anxiety he accomplished many things. He became a doctor and a scholar and a writer and an athlete, and he learned to play several instruments and to speak in several tongues. His mother admired scholarship, he told me once, and things "bellelitristic," and he wanted to please her because "his dumb brother never would."

It's not surprising, I guess, that such an attitude did not endear him to others, or that it took him a long time to marry, courting his mother again and again in the guise of other women. And then, to no one's surprise, he took a woman away from her husband and from her children too, because now that he was rich and famous, he was able to do what he's always wanted to do but couldn't when he was only three.

It takes many people a lifetime to begin to see the pattern to their lives and most never do. Which means that abandoned children remain abandoned, and victims cower on. And people who feel insecure as a child usually feel that way for some time more.

"None of us can help the things life has done to us. They're done before you realize it, and once they're done they make you do other things until at last everything comes between you and what you'd like to be, and you have lost your true self forever," Eugene O'Neill wrote. And maybe it was always thus, because patterns go on repeating like odd and even boards on a fence, and lovers search out needers, and losers look for winners, and people rarely change.

S̶ome say life is like a Greek tragedy, our doom apparent to all from the first scene. The script lying there on the table for anyone astute enough to read. Some feel we have work to do in this life left over from the one before. And those whom the gods take kindly to, they give a lot of pain, so that it will move them along faster to that place where they're meant to be. And there are those who believe that there are things that we must learn early on, which, if not learned then, hold us up in the next stage. I only know that we each are dealt a hand, and most of us seem to play it, and few of us think to say, "I don't want these cards" or "Could you deal again?"

I̶ know a girl whose mother died when she was small and whose father collapsed on her till she became parent to her father's child. She grew up feeling respected in return for forfeiting her right to depend, and she still denies her needs today while feeling angry deep inside.

There have been many reruns of this plot, and

many men who have helped her flesh out this already familiar story line. Ones who by their weaknesses made her feel strong. And those who watch from the outside wonder why such a smart girl would have such bad taste in men, never guessing that for her to try to accept love would be too terrifying, because it would remind her of when she was a child and felt afraid. And to try to trust again would bring the pain of too much need.

Some say anxiety is the spur that lures us on. The shade with whom we shadowbox all of our lives. And that we are drawn toward those things that make us anxious as a way of testing ourselves, so we draw near, and then rush off, until we exhaust ourselves.

There are those who say that once singed psychologically, the person so wounded must return to the scene of the crime, must play with the fire that burnt him, must live the scene out as many times as necessary until he can make it come out right. And like the gambler who must always roll once more, who can't cut his losses and give up the game, we continually try to rewrite the past while confirming it in our own minds.

"The Moving Finger writes; and having writ,/ Moves on:" Omar Khayyám told us in his *Rubáiyát*, and there are those who would say that he was right, that a role once chosen is rarely changed, and that most of us do not ask if we like the part we've got, even if it's a role we detest, we just ask ourselves how we might learn to play it with better grace.

Sometimes when you meet someone you can see the role they want you to play, and if it isn't one that fits your role, you might have to pass. Sometimes two givers will get together and have trouble meeting their own needs because both of them want to be the one who is needed and no one is available to be the one in need.

And sometimes a victim will meet another victim, and they'll fight for the right to be abused. Usually with the result that both will back off with revulsion, feeling furious with the other for trying to cast them in the role of the oppressor and for trying to keep all that moral indignation for themselves.

I knew a man once, and loved him too, who was determined to lose himself. And so we battled onward, I trying to love him into safety, he trying to shake me loose, until in time I realized he was winning, and if I did not set him free to do what he was determined to do, he would not just destroy himself, he would destroy me too.

And once a man came into my life, if just very briefly, who thought of himself as the adult in charge, and the minute he came in the door he began telling me what to do. "You will need a hat and a scarf," he'd say, "because it is very cold," and then he'd add, "I don't like that hat, wear the one you wore yesterday." By the end of a couple of weeks I could no longer think for myself, and if I'd kept seeing him, I wouldn't have been able to tie my shoes. But I misplaced him before that happened, couldn't wait, in fact, to slip him by, because I wasn't happy playing child to parent, it was a role I'd never known, although the part of parent to child had lines I could say by heart.

There are hero/prince scripts and loser/victim scripts, and villain/dragon scripts too, so some of us walk with grace upon this earth, and others hurl ourselves against it or lie down and wait for whomever to have their way with us.

Who is to say how it all happens? Is it imprint, or preference, fate, or vital design? I only know we all seem to pick a character to play in the comedy of life and stick with it through many acts. And whether we take it in with our mother's milk or choose it for ourselves, it seems to stay with us a long time, perhaps because it gives purpose to our lives.

There doesn't seem to be any connection between how you look and your success, or even how rich you are and how you feel about yourself, so there are beautiful people who are insecure and rich ones who have to buy friends. I've known very gifted people who go on auditioning all their lives and ones without a whole lot going for them who just assume the world will love them, and, oddly, it usually does.

"A cripple in the right way can beat a racer in the wrong" is the way Francis Bacon saw it, and there is no doubt he was right. It seems to be strictly a question of how you see yourself.

I once overheard a man in a restaurant telling a girl he was trying to impress the story of his life. "I was raised by lower middle-class parents," he said, "who wanted me to excel at any cost, with the result that I have strived all my life in several areas and made it to the top of none. And now I have arrived at this my advanced middle age," here he paused so that she could see he was still quite young, "and I am forced to admit, that in the world scheme of things, I am really only a mediocre economist. And as a linguist I have failed, as I speak only five or six tongues, and only three of those well. And I have never made it to Wimbledon, so I guess as a tennis player I do not rate. And even as a lover," here he smiled again and paused to assure her applause, "I must concede I am only fair." Then he looked at her winningly, hoping to get points for modesty, but she was too smart for him.

"We are coming at life from opposite ends," she told him. "I was raised by parents who thought I overachieved if I sucked my thumb, and, as a result, I am not even a mediocre economist, and in languages, I speak only one, and even a very poor tennis player would shun me on the courts, but you know, none of that bothers me a bit because I like myself."

# 3

## *Take what you want, said God, and pay for it*

I know an artist whose mother left home when he was small and who spent a good part of his childhood in a hospital looking out of the window and waiting for her to come back. He is an adult now, a bachelor and a man about town, and many would say a person who enjoys the good life. But those of us who have watched him over the years from the safe but helpless place of friendship know that it is no coincidence that he only falls in love with women who might leave their husbands or who are living out of town—or ones who are hung up on someone else but keep him just in case—and we suspect that their attraction is that he can wait for them as once he waited for his mother to come home.

Few of us know what toll we pay on the freight of unconscious wishes or how we make the thing that we fear the most knock upon our door or even how we might have lived our life if our life had not lived us.

There are many pages in the book, many kinds of lives we each can live, many ways to be rich, and even more to be poor. So there are those who would say we chose our own hell and, having chosen it, blame the gods. I only know that there are various kinds of pain out there all the time, and only certain kinds of it find their way to us.

I was at a party once at which a young bullfighter was also a guest, and everyone deferred to him and paid him court. Then finally, a woman, who had been most attentive, asked what was on everyone's mind. "You aren't afraid of anything, are you, Luis?" she said. "Yes I am," he answered. "I am afraid of bulls."

It does not surprise me that a man who feared bulls would spend his life facing that fear and staring it between the ears. We are all lightning rods with different frequencies, defying the gods to get us—and bargaining with them in the night.

Which, I guess, is why the person who feels powerless often finds a career like politics so he can renew his fears every election, and the person who fears rejection becomes an actor or a writer so he can do his death-defying act each and every review.

When you want to, there are many ways to give hostages to fortune, many ways to be sucked like a firefly into the flame, so those who fear abandonment find someone new to abandon them over and over again, and those who feel unworthy ask to be humbled, and the world always answers their prayers.

You can position yourself to get the kind of pain you want, and many of us do it very well, perfecting the art throughout our lives of our cruelty to ourselves.

I knew a man whose father was an alcoholic who, when drunk, was both fierce and unkind. And this man, who felt frightened as a boy because he could not protect himself or go to the aid of those he loved, still sets up his life today so he can feel powerless once more.

I could tell you how hard he works today to make sure he is abused, about how he's always several hours late, and the messy clothes he wears so he'll be despised, and how he squanders all his resources until he has to beg. And I could tell you how he lets down all the people who love him, so that he can feel guilty and unloved once again, but maybe it would be simpler to say instead that one of the ways to protect yourself from the monster is to become the monster yourself, and that's what happened to him.

The Hasidic Jews have a story about the Sorrow Tree. According to them, on Judgment Day, each person will be invited to hang from the Tree of Sorrows all of his own miseries, and that done, he will be given permission to walk around the tree and survey everyone else's miseries in order to select a set he likes better. According to Hasidic legend, each person then freely chooses his own personal set of sorrows once more.

"Take what you want," said God, "and pay for it," and many of us pay again and again. But how do we stop wanting what doesn't work for us? That's my question. And how do we learn to want something else?

Would that I knew for sure. I only know there are many levels of knowing and of learning and growing. And that being free is an inner state, and no one can take you there—you have to get there yourself.

And that there are no simple solutions to these problems, no spiritual road maps you can buy at a store. And that it doesn't matter if you are chained by a golden chain or an iron one if it holds you in a place that is doing you harm.

"A fatherless girl can only be satisfied with the heroic, the desperate, and the extreme," someone once said, meaning for me to hear. And with those words caused me to understand why for me all things are possible and nothing safe. Which isn't to say that action instantly followed insight, or that I do not still have to live along a distant day into the answer before I learn how to stop playing a lifelong game with the dark side of myself.

"An unexamined life is not worth living," Socrates said, so maybe all we can do is ask the right question and walk fast when the light at the end of the tunnel beckons to us. And choosing to be free is a step in the right direction. In fact, it is the first act in taking responsibility for your own life.

We are not prisoners, no traps or snares are set about us, but many of us imprison ourselves or at least are helplessly stalled. And some of us spend our lives staring into our navels and see nothing, and others cling to what robbed them and break their own hearts again and again. And some find gurus to lead them and wait for enlightenment to come. While others blame those who betrayed them while continuing the betrayal themselves.

There is a Buddhist parable about a young prince who completes his military studies under a renowned teacher and is accorded the title of Prince Five-weapons for his distinction, and armed with the five weapons so mentioned, he sets out on the road leading to the city of his father, the king.

On the way he comes to a forest. People at the mouth of the forest warn him not to enter the forest, telling him an ogre lives there named Sticky-hair who kills every man he sees. The young prince, confident in his training and hence fearless, enters the forest and in due time meets the ogre who engages him in battle. Each of the prince's weapons is soon rendered useless as the ogre, whose head is as big as a summer house, deflects each of them with his hair and they stick there. But after each weapon is immobilized, the prince challenges the ogre again, and finally the ogre says to him:

"Youth, why are you not afraid?"

"Ogre," the prince answers, "why should I be afraid? For in one life one death is absolutely certain. What's more I have in my belly a thunderbolt for a weapon."

And the ogre, understanding the weapon that the prince referred to as a thunderbolt was the Weapon of Self-Knowledge within him, let him go immediately, and the prince walked out of the forest a free man.

# Part Two
# SELF-AFFIRMA-TION

# No one ever
# loved anyone
# like anyone wants
# to be loved

A man I've known since childhood whose family fled Europe in the Holocaust once told me of being taunted for playing tennis by students when he first came to this country. "They thought it was a sissy's game because they all played football and basketball and baseball," he said, suntanned and handsome in his Brooks Brothers suit.

And then several months later, the same man became strangely evasive when I asked him how he was doing with his guitar lessons, and finally he acknowledged that he'd lost his guitar. Or rather that he'd left it in the subway, intending to go back and get it after a colleague from work, whom he'd spotted down the platform, got on a train. But someone who didn't share his ambivalence went off with it while he was trying to pretend he was someone other than himself.

A cat that sits down on a hot stove never sits on a stove again, but some of the stoves he doesn't sit on are not hot but cool. And it's equally true that where the tooth hurts the tongue always goes, and goes and goes again, until we stop the hurt.

Most of us can make jokes about the things that frightened us when we were small, raised as we all were in a Freudian world, in a world where people regularly brush their teeth in Narcissus' pool. But hurts once hurt do not get laughed away, and even those who laugh behind their hand when others acknowledge their deep fears, are often the killers of their own best dreams, and do not know they are.

I will acknowledge a kind of impatience myself, a wish to stop all this self-obsessing and get on with life. But I know no one goes forward who hasn't finished with the past, and those who try to, keep coming out the same door they went in.

Fears don't go away when they are ignored or when they are dismissed; they just go underground and fight a guerilla war deep inside our breasts, and we don't know we are possessed; we just go on dancing faster to contain our fright.

"A man is lonely till he finds himself," Ben Gurion once said, but where does one look? Ah, that's the rub. How does one find the place the knife went in?

I think one asks oneself what hurts, and when a new wound makes all the old ones ache, one asks if this is a movie one has already seen and if one really wants to keep on seeing it over and over again.

Psychiatrists talk of abandonment fears, and of feeling helpless or powerless, or of being rejected a lot, and maybe if you put all the fears in one pot and boiled them down, you would have two or three basic terrors and nobody would be immune. But some make better headway, the first wound never leaves entirely, perhaps, but we learn to walk with less of a limp, while others who wanted to fly get used to taking the train instead.

A television producer once told me of a relationship he had with a woman to whom he was very drawn and with whom he'd begun an affair. "The affair has fallen upon evil days," he said, looking embarrassed before he added, "I seem to have lost the urge. And yet I am clearly as in love with her as I ever was. I don't understand it," he said, shaking his head again. And then he added, as if in an aside, "Although it seems to have something to do with her dog." Questions about her dog produced no clarification, and we both gave up trying to understand the mysteries of the heart.

It was over a year later when I chanced to be looking through a family album with him that I saw a picture of the mother who had left him, when he was only three, sitting with him on her front porch beside a little gray dog, a dog just like the one owned by the woman he'd tried to love.

At some point we decide how conscious we want to be, how much truth we can take. And after that we chuck overboard the part of our subconscious that doesn't agree. Get rid of it, throw it into the sea. But because despair is anger with no place to go, pain that has gone inside and dug in deep, and because the body and the mind are not two separate things but only one, the mind's pain usually shows up somewhere else, so the search for self is a search for health.

Deep-seated fears go through several stages—anxiety is the first, then despair, and after that, denial or I don't care. But "I don't care" does not mean the fear is gone, only that the scar tissue has covered it up, and we can't see it anymore. Which is not to say we don't feel it anymore, but only when we do, we do not know what it is that hurts.

Denial of pain takes a lot of energy and requires the person to bankrupt himself mortgaging his fears. And when you divert energies to do the devil's work, you don't have it where you need it—you might not have much of it at all. Which means many of us spend our lives shunting back and forth between our pain and our defenses, pivoting on the promontory of our lives while we gaslight our dreams.

Many people push a burden of inexplicable sadness through a lifetime never gaining an understanding of the promptings of their hearts. They are always somehow still in transit, on the way but not knowing where they're going, only that they are as far as fulfillment is from longing and they have a long way yet to go.

"They can't scare me with their empty spaces," Robert Frost wrote. "I have it in me so much nearer home/To scare myself with my own desert places."

I had a friend once who had loved a Chinese girl and lost her in a tragic way, and after that, he avoided everyone who looked like her, preferring the company of big-busted blondes and usually ones who were married to someone else. A long while later he met a lovely girl who was slight of build and dark of hair, and he and she became friends but nothing more. And often he would remark, "It is too bad you aren't pretty" and tell her that "her scale was off," taking out his slide rule and measuring her as he talked. Because he'd always said, he told her, that if he ever met a girl who he could talk to as he talked to her, and who was pretty into the bargain, he'd marry her. She wondered often why he needed to tell her she wasn't up to his standards, and she understood that even if he honestly believed her to be deficient, it wasn't like him to be deliberately unkind. And once she even turned to him and said, "It may surprise you to learn that some people consider me pretty." But he only smiled, as if he couldn't imagine how she could believe the likes of them. And so they went on for many months, she offering love and he both seeking it and rejecting it. And then one day he invited her to his place, and there on the living room floor, she saw a number of collages he'd made with photos of her and Chinese memorabilia, and then she knew.

"These pictures," she said turning to him, "are not of me but of a memory. Somebody for whom you are saying a mass. Is it possible that you were once in love with a Chinese girl?"

He told her everything then, things he'd thought he'd stop remembering long ago, and in time he stopped running from himself.

There are two fears really. The original wound from way back when, and the fear of giving up our defenses and having to face the wild arrows of pain, so the fear becomes a roadblock that we service and maintain. Which is why those who cannot trust enough make sure they will not be trusted and those who fear most to be orphaned, widowed, or worthless, find themselves so, again and again.

"If, instead of Time's notorious and incompetent remedy, there was an operation," Cyril Connolly wrote in *The Unquiet Grave*, "by which we could be cured of loving, how many of us would not rush to have it! To be kept for six months in a refrigerator or to hibernate in deep narcotic sleep, to be given new drugs, new glands, a new heart, and then to wake up with the memory swept clear of farewells, and accusations, never more to be haunted by the grief-stricken eyes of our assassinated murders!"

Emotions rule all of us, even those who think they don't and the most ruled are those who've had to develop a large rational scaffolding to support their fears. Fears fight wars, and conquer worlds, build temples and bank accounts, get married and raise kids, but those who fear are always planning their defenses and their retreat, never living life, just escaping, never loving, only weeping.

We all carry the cross-hatching of a thousand wounds. The wounds of childhood, still bleeding like the signs of the stigmata. The wounds of adolescence, still stinging with remembered pain. The bitter wounds of adult failures, or soured loves and lost dreams.

How to make them all go away? How to become brave and young again? How to wipe the slate clean and reenter the world like a tabula rasa, trusting and trustworthy again? I wish I knew.

I only know the answer doesn't lie in learning how to protect yourself from life. It lies in learning how to strengthen yourself so you can let a bit more of it in.

"Why am I afraid to dance, I who love music and rhythm and grace and song and laughter?" Eugene O'Neill wrote in *The Great God Brown*. "Why am I afraid to live, I who love life and the beauty of flesh and the living colors of earth and sky and sea? Why am I afraid to love, I who love love? Why am I afraid, I who am not afraid? Why must I pretend to scorn in order to pity? Why must I hide myself in self-contempt in order to understand? Why must I be so ashamed of my strength, so proud of weakness? Why must I live in a cage like a criminal, defying and hating, I who love peace and friendship? Why was I born without a skin? O God, that I must wear armor in order to touch or be touched."

# 5

## *The wild arrows of pain*

I knew a woman once who was dying of a tragic disease, and after several years of lingering with her in the never-never land between life and death, her husband chose life and left.

It was a very hard decision for him to make, but he left nevertheless, and started a new life for himself, one that included children and a new wife. His former wife, left alone, had nothing left when he departed, nothing but her memories and her anger.

And every day the anger grew. She forbade her friends to see him, and she made everyone she knew choose between them and cut off those who would not censor him. Some days she spent all her energy dialing, with the pencil held between her teeth, the number of his office, so she could call him and complain, and other days she exhausted herself dictating her story into a tape recorder so that she could tell it to the world and make him an object of shame.

The nurses who looked after her hated to see her so upset and tried to calm her down, but she resisted all their efforts and continued to fan the flames. And finally, they came to understand that anger was all she had to live for, and it had become a substitute for love.

Anger is a passion, so it makes people feel alive and makes them feel they matter and are in charge of their lives. So people often need to renew their anger a long time after the cause of it has died, because it is a protection against helplessness and emptiness just like howling in the night. And it makes them feel less vulnerable for a little while.

I know a dancer who always chooses men who will somehow let her down— men who drink a lot, or who are mean to her, or who have one foot out the door—and when they do what anyone could see from the start was what they were likely to do, she always goes around in a rage, telling anyone who will listen how awful they have been.

There is a connection between anger and fear and sadness that is very strong, and it is easier for a lot of people to stay mad than to allow that nameless despair to rise up and take them over, so they bat it away with fury and keep on doing it as often as it takes.

In my memory, frozen frame, there is a series of emotional photographs of a young man I went to school with and parallel-marched alongside through many chapters of our lives. I remember him first when we were teenagers, and he was a student rebel who regularly defied the powers that be with his attacks on the system and his refusal to comply, and later as a political activist, as a writer, and as an intellectual, he did much the same thing.

The high school student who refused to sing the national anthem, or contribute to the student council because it was taxation without representation, became the adult who won prizes for his writing and turned them down or gave them away, the person who always pissed in the punch bowl at important occasions, and pointed out to others the absurdity of their lives.

"Love looks forward; hate looks back, and anxiety has eyes all over its head," or so Mignon McLaughlin wrote. And while one can never be very sure why someone might solicit and then reject that which they want most, sometimes when a child doesn't get what he needs when he is small an anger develops deep within him because he feels unsupported, and hence frightened and alone. And because the road between fear and hate is such a short one, many people travel over it without ever leaving home.

There is a story from the seventeenth century about Walter Raleigh and his son who fell to arguing in a tavern. Walter hit his son a severe blow to the side of his head. The boy teetered about stunned for a moment, then fell back in a chair at a table of some strangers. For a moment he appeared stunned, then hauled off and punched the man sitting next to him saying, "Box about, t'will come to my father anon," which, I guess translated from the Elizabethan, must mean something like, "Pass it on. Sooner or later it will get back to my dad."

"Sons of the thief, sons of the saint. Who is the child with no complaint?" the Jacques Brel song goes. And even when the father who has failed us is several wretched valleys on, and we cannot remember any longer when we became an orphan or who first let us down, we still feel the rage.

There is nothing new about any of this, of course. Angers have been known to resonate, and abuse to be a form of homage, and hurts intended for another have been delivered to the door of someone else, from the dawn of time, and they always will.

We all need love, and want it, and fear to get it too. Fear that if it comes to us it might hurt us, or that even believing in it, is to accept our need for it and give it power over us. So many people spend their lives trying to dissuade themselves of their needs, and they ask for love in a thousand places and spit to windward when it answers their call.

One could make a pretty good case for most angers resulting from unmet needs to be parented, which is why so many lives become addenda to their own first years. And why so many people use themselves up playing picador or bull-fighter still smarting from the love that went unde-livered. And others put themselves under house arrest and spend their days dimming their lights for someone who didn't manage to love them enough.

Dependency always makes you feel angry, whether it is physical, financial, or emotional, because dependency makes you feel vulnerable, and vulnerability makes us feel afraid. And few of us seem to have the personal ballast not to fear we will be fumbled, not to need to armor ourselves against the terrors and anxieties that bind us to our past.

Some people who are angry turn their anger on themselves, and some project it outward on whoever's going by, and some find a cause for it, a vehicle that makes it safe, and some banish those who are loved, or torture those whose vulnerability reminds them of their own.

Guilt is anger at oneself, and masochism is anger turned against oneself because to express it directly carries too many risks. And passive hostility is sniping from behind a tree and looking the other way. There are many kinds of anger, expressed many kinds of ways, from envy to resentment to jealousy to blame—all ways we have invented to hide from ourselves our lack of courage to grieve.

Psychiatrists would say that anger is preferable to sadness because it gets the pain moving, gets it stirring about. And I suppose that is true. But nothing much is accomplished if we stay angry all of our lives, and if anger becomes a snare in which we lay caught, or if our hatred makes us an occupied country, a fortress we've built ourselves and from which we can't get out, and if we quiver there recounting everyone's misdeeds, never getting a purchase on our life, a victim of another victim, a continuum into time.

I know, and so do you, many people who have been badly hurt, and that hurt goes back so far, the people dealing with them today can't see the wound anymore, and neither perhaps can they. A widow who is old and frightened now and furious at her husband for dying and leaving her unprotected takes it out on her children who, she feels, have neglected her no matter what they do. A widower, who is still angry that his wife left him with several kids to raise, so punishes all the women whom he meets who don't somehow fill her shoes. A bachelor, angry at his mother for reasons he no longer remembers, passes his days going in and out of sulks, and often when he finds a woman who might make it all up to him, he punishes her in bed. And when he holds her hand, he just happens to twist her wrist, or bend her fingers back. Or maybe he simply defaults in little ways—always forcing her to do for him, never doing for her—and when she complains, he just smiles and, lying back in the bushes, looks the other way.

So, many of us sit about the rubble, picking shards from broken lives out from under our skin, talking wretchedly of famine, vexed and chafing with our own abandonment, counting the many treasons and deceptions while we tie ourselves tighter to the tether and turn the winch ourselves.

Some say we read the world wrong and say it deceives us, and others that anger is the hate that bruises, even though the heart is braced. And both of them are right. Mistrust becomes a self-fulfilling prophesy, and until you let it go, you can't go anywhere yourself.

As long as you blame someone it makes the problem not yours but theirs, and allows you to keep it without taking responsibility for anything but pointing the finger. Which means you give them responsibility for your life and paralyze yourself forever in a place you don't want to be. And there you sit—waiting for justice, waiting for someone to save you, waiting for your mother to kiss it and make it all better, waiting for Godot. And you continue to feel powerless, and helpless, and frightened and angry, and things remain just as they were.

I know a girl who was the fifth of five daughters in a family in which a son was definitely sought, and shortly after her first birthday, one finally did arrive. The girl whom I know grew up feeling like an accessory after the fact, a kind of unnecessary item that no one really cared about, and over the years her anger grew and grew, although it was never directly expressed to them or to herself.

For many years she perceived her life in the flawed light of love and grief, committing doubtful acts of all descriptions, and always seeking to abdicate and force someone to mother her. She moved away from home as soon as she was able and did not speak to her parents from then on but found substitutes for them in countless others. And fresh loves betrayed her every day as she endured on, squirming in the caressing grip of her rage, always able to conjure up another set of unique defeats.

One of the things that often came up when she talked to others about her childhood was the five fine gold pocket watches her father had bought as gifts when his daughters were small for his future sons-in-law. The watches were to her a symbol for the value her parents put on males, even males they'd never met, as well as a symbol of how little value they put on the daughters they had born, and especially on herself, the overrun.

Four of the watches found their way in time into the possession of sons-in-law, but the pocket watch intended for her future husband lay in its box for more than thirty years. And then one day when misfortune forced her back to her parents' home for a little while, she asked about it, and it was withdrawn and brought forth. She saw it glittering there in her father's hand, mocking her for not being a man, and mocking her for not producing a man to be her father's son-in-law as her sisters had done, and then she knew: "I have not married all these years," she told herself, "because I have not wanted to bring home a son-in-law for him and have him pass me up again." And knowing that, she was able to learn from the past and walk away from it at last.

"Motives, like stowaways, are found too late," Auden said, and it was ever thus. Who is to say who did what to whom, or how much we did to us? I only know a lot of people hate those who failed them once, and hating them hate themselves, and anger becomes their defense and their sentence, their protest and their prayer.

# 6

## *It doesn't matter if you are chained by a golden chain or an iron one*

I worked with a man once who was always looking for another hit of self-esteem. He tried designer's clothes and one-night stands, and weeks at Club Med and going to est, and girls with silicone breasts and publishing his own books, and he dropped the names of his celebrity friends and overtipped head waiters.

He tried fame, and getting rich, pedigree dogs and country clubs, dropping out and buying in, meditating and thinking thin. He even tried renouncing his religion and joining Zen, but nothing ever worked.

If, by "worked," one means helping him to love himself.

It sounds funny when you tell it, but it's not so funny when you live it, and many people do. Spurred on by the North American motto, "If you're not number one, why bother?" and our fears that "they" are gaining on us, those siblings who once tailgated us long ago, we search everywhere for the love that eluded us when we were young and find it not.

Psychologists would say our sense of impotence, or need to show the world, is caused by an undeveloped psyche and shows we are still at the first stage of our development. Stuck with the infant's dream of omnipotence, we try to invent the breast with our cries. And sociologists would say our society is still very young, so there are those who think that safety can be found by hedging oneself behind a wall of possessions, and have not yet learned that having can get in the way of being, and that one can never buy oneself. I can only say that a lot of people position themselves outside the charmed circle and struggle their whole life to get in, while others stand on the outside throwing rocks at those inside. And most of the time, the battle is not with the people who they want to join, or feel won't let them in, the battle is with themselves.

I knew a girl, when I was in school, who was always in despair every time she got a paper back and found her mark was only a B-plus and not the A she sought, and everybody watched her slink away and assumed that she had failed, and perhaps they were right, because not topping the class was to her a failure of a terrible sort.

She was a pretty girl and a very smart one too, but that was never enough. The only thing she knew was that her parents always made it clear that they thought her older sister was the one with brains and she the one with looks, and she was trying to prove them wrong. And she never understood that it was because her sister was not as fair of face that they gave her the identity that they did, she only knew she'd been passed by in some essential way, and feeling inadequate became the pattern of her life.

For many of us self-hate is the result of an ancient but still nagging sting, a sad echo of an earlier bruise from which we never seem to recover, and so we keep ourselves auditioning, always remaining a seeker in another's land, the person who shouts across the gulf, hoping to be heard.

Some say those who constantly hear the call to prove or improve, whose script in life is number two and trying harder, or pretty good but no cigar, are children of overly critical parents, or parents who were indifferent in the extreme. But my guess is that narcissism plays a big part as well, and that our tendency to set impossible standards for ourselves, and our contempt for ourselves for not being rich and successful or beautiful beyond compare come from our sense that we should be privileged or, one might say, from our repressed longing for unconditional love.

Because it is just a hop and a skip and a jump between lack of self-esteem to self-hate to self-obsession, and when you are continually seeking the privileged place of the favored child, you are trading off acceptance of yourself as you actually are for an idealized image of the person you wish you were, which means judging yourself by higher standards than you'd set for anyone else. So you're always finding yourself wanting, always letting yourself down, and your overblown ego always lets you know.

There was a wonderful line in a novel I once read that went, "Edith was a little country bordered on the north, south, east, and west by Edith," and that pretty well sums it up. The self-obsessed person lives in a house with mirrors instead of windows, seeing himself at every glance. So he is always the observer, always the censor, and for him there is little relief from the torment of self-doubt because shame darts in all his unguarded gateways and false pride opens his doors.

It's a pity that anyone should spend his or her life agonizing over being a misfit when we are all misfits after all. In fact, one could say such people are giving themselves airs and that failure has gone to their heads. And if it is possible to be vain about one's shortcomings, then that's what they are about.

The self-centered person is an emotional hypochondriac always checking the pulse of his feelings. And sounding the depths of his grief, and his competitiveness, his perfectionism, as well as his constantly calling up of guilt-ridden memories to flagellate himself are symptoms of his disease. And he never overcomes his dependency on others' approval or his need to exploit others to make up for his sense of inadequacy and to give himself a sense of worth.

In that long ago when being was believing, a young poet once married a struggling actress, the girl of his dreams, a soul mate who would help him live out his potential, a muse who would inspire him and be by his side while he worked, giving him loving support and for whom he could write parts in his plays.

After two years his new wife fell short of the poet's dream of perfection. Concerned about her own fledgling career, she would leave the house some evenings when her husband was working and make the rounds of the agents, producers, and show parties, looking for parts. Enraged at her unfaithfulness, the poet accused her of selfish behavior and hinted that her interest in these outings was sexual, not professional. Inflamed by jealousy, he spent his days in towering rages, sulking and hysterical and when his wife tried to work things out, he turned his back on her. Within six months he had found a companionable ear to tell his troubles to. A pretty young woman who catered the pastries in his neighborhood café listened as he poured out his sad tale of his wife's many cruelties and how she broke his heart. And before too much longer he and his new friend ran off to Europe. He left his wife a note telling her only that he was leaving her and that he had found his dream girl at last.

He and the pastry cook settled into a flat in London where he worked on his plays while she cooked wonderful meals for the two of them in the kitchen. For a while they were happy, then she began to miss her friends, and hoping to set up a small catering company again, she began to visit the local cafés in the afternoon. Soon the recriminations started. Her hopes for a career were ruining their marriage. Her part of the bargain was to provide love and support—he would supply the money and the glory. His new wife began to drink to drown out his attacks. Before long, on a trip back to North America, he found someone who understood him. A beautiful dancer he met at a party listened to his tales of broken dreams and perfidy. She was moved by his passion as he wept at the lost possibilities. "He could have given her everything, if only she was more worthy of his love." He moved in with the dancer, "just until he got his broken heart together." By the end of the week he wired his wife, telling her to see her lawyer and to say he would not be back. That was three years ago, and his third marriage is over as well—but not his demands for total devotion, not his clamoring for self-importance, not his need for someone to make him feel valuable or his sense of being valueless when they take their attention from him for a moment. And his life is still in others' hands.

When you don't love yourself, you are always at the mercy of those who might do the job, never your own person, always theirs. And your emotional center of gravity is always very shaky, causing you to make your own turmoil wherever you go and to befog your experience, believing it them.

Other people in such hands simply become instruments that work or do not serve you well, and not people in their own right or people with needs of their own. So there are a lot of people saying "choose me or lose me" to people who say

"I choose myself" because no one wants to be an extension of another; everyone wants to be loved for himself.

It has been said that there are four stages of the soul, the baby stage when one thinks the whole world is oneself, the infant stage when it becomes a world of me and non-me. The stage of the child when it is me and you, and with that the idea that I can make you into me. And the final stage of adulthood when it is you and me and that includes the idea that I am you, which is to say, part of a larger whole. And if one looks at life that way, many of us still have a way to go. And all those who think in terms of disposable people, or assign to others roles and play themselves off the villains and the dragons and the princesses that they've set up, have got some homework yet to do. And the place that they must start is where one learns to accept oneself.

A woman I know once told me a touching story about a picture frame she'd bought when she was still quite young, and about a spell the woman in the store put on it, and her, by saying,

"Keep it for a picture of your own true love, but be sure that he is true."

"I first put a picture of a man I was seeing in it," she said, "but dashed it when we were through. Then I put my mother's picture in it because my psychiatrist told me what I wanted from men was what I never got from her." Then she said, looking somehow younger than her years, "And these days I've got a mirror in it, having decided I am the only one I can count on to love me for myself. But I haven't figured out how to do that yet. I just hope I will learn to do so soon."

"The real voyage of discovery consists not in seeking new landscapes but in having new eyes," Marcel Proust wrote, and, of course, only too many of us get too soon old and too late smart, always hungering for something further away or long ago, or still about to be, while everything we need resides within.

There is a Hasidic story about a very poor rabbi named Rabbi Eizik, son of Yekel of Cracow, who dreamed that someone bade him look for a treasure under a bridge leading to the king's palace in Prague. When the dream reappeared for the third time, Rabbi Eizik set out for Prague. But the bridge was guarded day and night, and he dared not arouse suspicion by digging so he waited, walking around the bridge from sunrise to sundown. Finally, the captain of the guards asked if he could help him. Rabbi Eizik, seeing he was a kindly man, told him about his dream and how he had come all this way from a distant country. The captain laughed. "So to please a dream you have worn out all that shoe leather and come all this way," he said to Rabbi Eizik. "If I had as much faith in my dreams as you have in yours, I would have gone to Cracow to look for treasure under the stove of a Jew named Rabbi Eisik, son of Yekel. Wouldn't I have been a fool?"

Rabbi Eizik thanked him for his trouble, bowed, traveled home, dug up the treasure under his stove, and built a house of worship with the money. So that every day he could thank God for helping him to understand his treasure was not in some distant place but in the place where he stood every day— which is to say wherever he himself was.

*Part Three*

# SELF-
# HEALING

# Unwind the
# solemn twine

I went to school with a boy whose family fell from grace when his father, a corporation president, lost his job. The young man I knew was then an adolescent, and it was perfect timing in some ways for him to slide sideways into his Bohemian period, to do a barefoot poet, a student radical, denying his needs as if it were a virtue, and for a while to confuse himself into believing that he was still intact. But soon the sixties evaporated, and so did his youth, and the ruptures in his psyche began to appear more and more transparent even to him.

He had by this time developed a series of contradictions. He had champagne tastes, but considered himself a Marxist. He had worked very hard to acquire a professional degree, but preferred to work as a laborer. He was drawn to upper-class girls, but treated them badly—perhaps because they had what he did not—and usually managed to get himself rejected before very long. Occasionally, he met a girl who loved him for what he really was, but he always looked on girls like this as if they were a weakness in himself, and turned them down. He didn't want to be loved for what he really was. He preferred his fantasy of himself. The vision of himself as someone evicted from the Garden of Eden, someone doomed to walk the earth alone, unloved, unheralded, and unknown.

The conflict between what one is and who one is expected to be touches all of us. And sometimes rather than reach for what one could be, we choose the comfort of the failed role, preferring to be the victim of our circumstances, the person who didn't have a chance. I sometimes think we fall in love with the fantasy of ourselves as a doomed creature and like our fantasy more than we like ourselves.

It's the Woody Allen special. "I'm sophisticated. I'm intellectual. I've got angst."

"All neurotics are either Oedipus or Hamlet," Freud said, and maybe he was right, because there does seem to be a scarcity of plots when it comes to trauma, and all roads do seem to lead to Mom.

"Whales branded in the Arctic are found swimming in the North Atlantic, but men ringed in childhood are found in old age under the same stone," Cyril Connolly wrote in *The Unquiet Grave*, a book he called "an exercise in self-dismantling." And that is, of course, the task at hand. Because denial can follow you to the grave if you let it, and it is so easy to do so, easier by far than to face yourself squarely and give up your games.

The old thrill and the old despair—how real they seem, how intimate and strangely comforting. "What are you doing about what bothers you?" we ask ourselves. "Perhaps it is not too late." But somehow it is easier to continue to deceive oneself, to let the blood quicken in the old familiar ways.

"Insecurity is the negative expected," someone once said, and that is certainly true. We see the world through our insecurities and fit our truth to them, and because our blindness has been with us for as long as we can remember, it is the only truth we know.

There is a part in Plato's *Republic* in which Plato asks his students to imagine a group of people imprisoned in an underground cave in such a way that they can see only each other's shadows and hear the shadow of each other's voices.

"These are strange prisoners," remarks one of Plato's students.

"Like ourselves," answers Plato. "To them the truth is but the shadow of the images."

$A$re we all walking around in an illusionary reality seviced by our own limited vision, a world we recreate every day from our own thought system? None of us wants to believe it's so, and yet it is.

How do some people give themselves the slip and come out of the dark tunnel into the light of day, and others play the same game all their lives, losing to themselves each and every day? Is it simply an ability to recognize patterns? An accident of genetics? A couple of cells of gray matter more or less in the right place? Perhaps, but I think not. It's more a matter of how soft the flesh in which the knife was plunged. How deep the thrust. And by whom.

$M$y own pain seems to rise within me, whenever anyone tries to care for me, to parent me, as once long ago my father did. And should they offer love and protection, and I find the courage to lay my burden down, and then they withdraw it, my stomach falls right through me, and I begin to shake.

If you were to see me on a sunny day, with my friends around me and a smile upon my face, you would never guess. I can handle hurts of many kinds, and challenges galore. It's kindness I have trouble with, and tenderness from someone I could love that always makes me cry. I suppose the joy reminds.

There is a story in the "Third Night" of the *Book of The Thousand and One Nights* about a Jinni whom a fisherman lets out of a jar of yellow copper, only to be told the following:

"I am one of the heretical Jinni, and I rose against Solomon son of David (on the twain be peace!). I was defeated. Solomon son of David bade me embrace the Faith of God and obey his behests. I refused. The king shut me up in this copper recipient and impressed on the cover the Most High Name, and he ordered the submissive Jinni to cast me into the midmost of the ocean. I said in my heart: 'Whoso shall release me, him I shall make rich forever.' But an entire century passed, and no one set me free. Then I said in my heart: 'Whoso shall release me, to him shall I reveal all the magic arts of the earth.' But four hundred years passed, and I remained at the bottom of the sea. Then I said: 'Whoso releases me, him will I give three wishes.' But nine hundred years passed. Then, in despair, I swore by the Most High Name: 'Whoever will set me free, him will I slay. Prepare to die, O my savior!' "

Mortal wounds, once sustained but never healed, are like bound feet. One does not notice how much they hurt until someone takes the bindings off, and then the pain is great. And sometimes we make the mistake of running from the person who removes the bindings rather than from the one who put them on.

I had a very wise high school teacher years ago who once told this story on herself. She was driving home one day when an abandoned tricycle blocked her path. She got out of her car to move it and was surprised to find a rage building up inside her.

"Damn kid," she said to herself, "doesn't deserve a bike if he can't look after it. Somebody should teach him a lesson or two. I feel like taking this blinking bike and hurling it over the bridge or something."

Then she burst out laughing. "Kathryn," she said aloud to herself, standing in the middle of the suburban street, "if you want a bloody tricycle so badly, why don't you buy yourself one." Then she laughed again because she knew why she resented that kid with the tricycle. And the reason was very simple. She envied him!

He had the shiny new trike her impoverished childhood had never lavished on her. He had it, and he didn't even know how lucky he was. Should not the gods strike him dead?

Unexpected emotions are a good way to figure out what hurts. Tempers that flare about unimportant things, tears that appear at odd times when we don't expect them, tell us what we feel even when we aren't telling ourselves. I once broke into tears in a movie, a comedy about a group of dogs who apprehended a ring of burglars. When the lawyer, asked by the judge if he represented the dogs, replied, "No, your Honor, these dogs acted on their own responsibility," everyone in the movie theater roared but me. I sat there and cried. And nobody needed to tell me why it was I did—the answer was writ loud and clear. I identified with those dogs, because like them I had no one to accept responsibility for me. A situation that, however much I might prefer to keep it from myself, was causing me considerable pain. My tears made it clear I'd had it up to here with being brave.

Very often in life the defenses we set up to make us feel in charge of our life, the controls if you will, take over our life and control us. And in time we can't get past our own front lines.

Our North American culture, more than any other, thrusts independence on us at an early age, and needs for community and affection and dependence are sacrificed to the god of standing tall.

Which means that a lot of people who needed to be protected when they were small got pushed from the nest too soon and had to learn to look after themselves. But often what they learned to protect themselves from was their own needs, needs that were never wrong.

The existentialists say all our fears are but the one fear of our death because the inevitability of death underlines our powerlessness and the meaninglessness of life, and all the fears we acknowledge to ourselves are just metaphors for that big dread. And oedipal complexes and penis envy and sibling rivalry and fears of abandonment and all the rest are simply confrontations with our fears of being powerless—assaults to our self-esteem. And the lies we tell ourselves are necessary to protect us, to keep submerged the terrible truth, the knowledge we don't want to have. The fact is that whatever we want to believe about ourselves, the real truth is we are but a grain of sand.

There is a lot of truth in what they say—that we

develop our defenses to comfort ourselves, and that's I guess why I persist in asking the question I must ask. Do our defenses comfort us? Or hinder us? Do we still need the limp? Because if the limp is causing new aches or keeping the original wound unhealed and making it reverberate, we'd be better off without it.

"The greatest discovery of my generation is that human beings by changing the inner attitudes of their minds can change the outer aspects of their lives," William James said, which is to say it is up to you. Are you going to remain alone with the apparatus of blame, with all your lies unredeemed, with what you have to offer in a locked room, lying in wait for tomorrow? Or are you going to ransom today and make it yours?

Some defense systems are part of the problem and some are part of the solution. And what we need to ask is this: Is ours defending us from hurts, or keeping us from what we need? Are we inside the prison of our defenses, or are we outside walking on the wall looking out to sea?

There is a Greek myth about Ariadne, the daughter of King Minos of Crete, who fell in love with Theseus, one of the group of

Athenian youths who were to be thrown into the labyrinth to feed the minotaur. Ariadne sought the help of Daedelus by whose art the labyrinth was originally constructed, and begged him to help her save Theseus. The crafty Daedalus presented her with a skein of linen and bade her have Theseus fix it to the entrance and unwind it as he went into the maze.

It was so little that was needed to save Theseus, but the little was at hand, and the little is at hand for you and I as well. Where our pain is, that's where our life is, and we can follow it like a skein of linen thread, and it will lead us out of the labyrinth and back home again.

"When you ask what love is," said Krishnamurti, "you may be too frightened to see the answer. . . . You may have to shatter the house you have built, you may never go back to the temple. . . Fear is not love," he said. Nor is love dependence, jealousy, possessiveness, domination, responsibility, duty, self-pity, or any of the other things that conventionally pass for love. "If you can eliminate all these, not by forcing them but by washing them away as the rain washes the dust of many days from a leaf, then perhaps you will come upon this strange flower which man always hungers after."

# *It is better to light candles than to curse the darkness*

I have a friend whose infant brother was killed in a freak accident when she was just three. And her parents blamed her because it was easier than blaming themselves, and then they banished her, claiming they could not stand to be reminded of what had been. She grew up in a convent and then in a foster home and absorbed a lot of guilt about being a bad child. She is remarkably free of the anger you would expect to attend that kind of plot, but I can always see her pain. And it shows itself most clearly when she runs to the rescue of someone else—she having learned long ago that one of the best ways to stop feeling hard-done-by is to rescue someone else.

"Each man is haunted until his humanity awakens," is what Blake said. And it would be hard to disagree with him, because one of the best ways there is to nourish yourself is to nourish others, and many people have walked across that bridge and found themselves home at last.

There are many parts in the play of life, of course, and some who feel themselves victims deep down inside don the persecutor's cloak as time goes by and, instead of liberating themselves by saving others, take their revenge instead, and because love is as love does, they find it not.

And still others wear the martyr's robe and wallow in their pain, and no one can ever make it up to them, or they save themselves. And some put on the narcissist's dress and try to love themselves without realizing the shortest distance between two points is not always a straight line, and when it comes to finding love, a circle does it best.

I know there are those who would say that the person who rescues others in order to save himself is not out of the woods yet, and like the atheist who is a god-involved man, he is simply running the same movie through again, but this time in reverse. But I don't really agree because it appears to me that there are irritants in all of our lives, and some people make a pearl of them, while others only cry, and those who love out their hurts leave them behind—them and a better world.

There is an old rabbinic tale, which goes: And the Lord said to the Rabbi, "Come, I will show you hell." They entered a room where a group of people sat around a huge pot of stew. Everyone was famished and desperate. Each held a spoon that reached the pot but had a handle so long it could not be used to reach their mouths. The suffering was terrible.

"Come, now I will show you heaven," the Lord said after a while. They entered another room, identical to the first—the pot of stew, the group of people, the same long spoons. But there everyone was happy and nourished. "I don't understand," said the Rabbi. "Why are they happy here when they were miserable in the other room, and everything was the same?" The Lord smiled. "Ah, but don't you see?" He said. "Here they have learned to feed each other."


There is something about life in North America—the "We do it all for you society"—that makes everyone feel in need, and no one feel as if he has anything to give. So, we are a culture in which love is in short supply, and consumers fight for the little there is of it as if they were at a sale.

We are a culture that equates productivity with making lots of money, and we don't concern ourselves with the production of psychological goods of any kind. So we live in a world where loneliness is epidemic, a world of users where no one wants to be used.

We are a people who rush about passively seeking, a people who make a busyness of our needs. Others must service us, stimulate us, entertain and inform us, even feed and love us, and the husks of the many we have sucked dry and shed, lie scorned in our wake, hoping for someone else to come along and resurrect them.

We live in a world that would rather watch, a world of parentless children who have never been weaned. And we stand, as if instructed, in the foyer of our lives, waiting for the coup de foudre, the thunderbolt, that will open the door for us—not understanding the promise is only a promise unless we translate it into treasure. Unless we pick up our power and grope our way to adulthood, we will always wait.

Some people think they can find happiness by stockpiling possessions and stubbornly try to wrest fulfillment from the accumulation of things, and others look for themselves in others' bodies or seek direction for their lives in horoscopes and drugs.

And some think glory will do it and try to find a little self-respect in the repetition of their names as it falls from strangers' lips.

And some become narcissists and attempt to love themselves by covering their self-hate with the costume of self-love while the gifts of others go unnoticed and hang suspended in space, and they spar with the seeping-creeping conviction that nothing really matters and that there is no hope.

But this I can tell you true—until you divest yourself of the notion that you are a collection of needs, an empty vessel that someone else must fill up, there will be no safe place to harbor yourself, no safe shore to reach. As long as you think mostly of getting, you will have nothing real to give.

There was a man once who sought power, thinking it would somehow protect him from the things that go bump in the night, but on the way to power he made many others feel powerless, so the armies trying to finish him off grew larger every day. He did not understand that he was bringing this about and grew more fearful and more fierce, more powerful and more powerless, and every day, the step he took in the direction he thought forward thrust him back in space.

There's a woman, too, who gets drunk and abusive at parties and talks endlessly, keeping others from exchanges of their own with her constant bids for their attention and her hostilities not so carefully veiled. And usually her evenings end in disaster, and the next morning she must make several calls. "Do you know when you drink, you get a little hostile?" is what she usually says.

I don't know why it isn't more obvious to more of us more of the time that those who fear get someone to be afraid of, and those who wish to be angry need simply step out on the street and yell to find someone out there who will curse right back at them. Because what you put energy into comes toward you, and what you select is what you get. Just as what you want to see your eyes fall on, and what you expect to be told arrives for you to hear.

There are many lessons to be learned from nature, many messages like cookie crumbs scattered about the path waiting to be picked up and followed home again by anyone who heeds them there. And one of them surely is the sound that comes back to us when we holler in a valley or shout in a forest, which is to say, the cadences of our own voice telling us again what we told it. Because all that we send into the lives of others comes back into our own, just as by our actions we create the world we live in, and what we send into the world is out there to greet us on the morrow when we go out to see. And while there are many filters that fractionalize our field of vision, and many hands clasped over our ears, we can't assume our response is not necessary. Everything is always out there, and it is we, and only we, who are the creators of our lives.

We are our choices and our choices not made. We are what we do and what we do not do as well. Just as surely as we are what is done to us, although many people talk about all that has befallen them without asking themselves how much of it was brought about by them.

The roots of love sink down deep and strike out far, and they are arteries that feed our lives, so we must see that they get the water and sun they need so they can nourish us. And when you put something good into the world, something good comes back to you.

I wish I knew what makes it possible for some of us to trip the switch one day and leave the world of longing and loss and enter one that is alive and yearning. I only know it has something to do with making an offering to the lifeforce, something to do with feeling your own power through its direct use. And I know, as certainly as I can, that life will continue to suck at you like an undertow as long as you walk the tightrope of your emotions, producing nothing but your fears.

And while I can not promise that no one will want any longer if he acts instead of waits, if he thinks other instead of self, if he gives forth instead of trying to fill up—I can tell you this, one hears the voice of becoming only in conversation with another, and only in reaching out of oneself to touch another person do we feel the fingers of love stroking us.

Some people say if others won't give it to me, I won't give it to anyone else, and some say if no one will give it to me, I will go without, but there is another answer simple as it can be. If no one will give to me, I will give to them. And in being the creator, I will create myself.

It is better to light candles than to curse the darkness. It is better to plant seeds than to accuse the earth. The world needs all of our power and love and energy, and each of us has something that we can give. The trick is to find it and use it, to find it and give it away, so there will always be more. We can be lights for each other, and through each other's illumination we will see the way. Each of us is a seed, a silent promise, and it is always spring.

# 9

## *Compassion is the thing that leads you gently back to yourself*

There is an apocryphal story about a man who turned to God one night when he was sorely tried and called out, "When can I stop giving, God? I haven't anything more to give!"

"You can stop giving when I stop giving to you," came the answer.

"When you stop giving to me!" the man cried out, enraged, thinking of his son who was fatally ill and his ex-wife who made his life miserable, and even of his friends who loved him but could do nothing for him in his pain—and only stood by feeling impotent, or worse ran from him out of weakness and fright and had to be consoled. "All you are giving me is pain and sorrow."

"No, that isn't right," came the answer. "I gave you life, and that is my gift, a pearl of great price. The pain and sorrow are another matter. But since you brought them up, they have made you a strong man, don't you agree? Would you rather be a weaker man, perhaps a man like one of your friends who is less certain of his strength because he has always been given to?"

"Since you put it that way," said the man, feeling chastened, "I would like to thank you for the gift of my life and for helping me develop the strength to be a giver. I realize now that it is a privilege to be able to give and will complain no more."

So many of us spend our life feeling hard-done-by, thinking that we have been unfavorably dealt with by fate or family and friends. Or that we did not get enough, whatever enough is, that we received less than our due, as if there was a due recorded somewhere that everyone had a right to, and that they issued at a store. And we never understand how lucky we are, or how much we have to give, only that the world's against us, and that life is hard.

I don't know why this is, or why for some it isn't. Nor do I know where some get that largeness of spirit, that bigness of soul that makes them able to reach inside of themselves and give and give again.

And others, lacking the bold heart and the firm step, remain in their jail and curse the gods. I only know that if you don't find the courage to give compassion, you'll have to find the courage to live without it. Because I am as certain as I can be that those who don't give it, don't get it, and that's as firm a law of nature as there is. And that in the unknown depth of spirit where strange things are stowed away, where we have our ghosts in boxes, and compassion's locked up tight, there is one door marked "open" and another door marked "shut," and the key to both is in our heart, and there is only one.


In that time long ago when divorce was thought to solve problems, there was a man who had a daughter and a wife who was no longer his. He could not forgive his wife for not loving him enough, and when his little girl came to live with him and his new wife he asked that she tell no one that she had another mother somewhere but allow everyone to think instead that she was the child of her stepmother and himself. The little girl was very troubled by her father's request, but she tried to do his bidding, finding her heart hardening against her stepmother instead of opening to take her in. Finally, she asked her real mother what to do.

"Now that you are living with your father and his new wife," her mother said, "you will find that she will do many of the things for you that I used to do. And when this happens, you will come to love her and to want to call her mother. And if that is the case it will not be wrong, or vex me, because no one can have too many people in their life who love them, only not enough."

The little girl felt better after her mother said this, but there was something in her father's insistence that she not tell anyone about her past or her other home in another city or ever speak of her real mother, whom she loved, that made her very sad, and she grew sick.

The father grew very angry when his child was ill and blamed his former wife for not giving her the care she needed when she was small, and he blamed his new wife for not being as good a mother as she should be, but he never questioned himself. Finally, his former wife, seeing the little girl suffering, wrote her husband-who-once-was a note, trying to speak as gently as she could. "To ask our daughter to turn her back on her mother is to ask her to renounce herself, just as to teach her disloyalty to one person is to teach her disloyalty to all. And while I know your purpose," she continued, "in asking her to not mention me is to give your new wife the respect you feel her sacrifice deserves, I am afraid that to force this on the child, rather than wait for her to accept her second mother out of love, will cause a breach and not a bond." And the father, realizing she was right, stopped trying to show his former wife how much better he was than she, or how easily she could be replaced, and he began to try to understand that there was enough love in the world and in his little girl's heart for all of them, and soon there really was.

Compassion can't exist with anger or jealousy, with envy or revenge, so those who have those feelings starve themselves. In the hands of the insecure, compassion becomes condescension, competitiveness, pity, and a taste for pain. Real compassion comes from strength. And when it comes from weakness it is another thing. Real compassion means feeling with, not feeling superior or feeling right, and you can't have it for others when you don't have it for yourself.

Some people think they are loving others when they are only demanding love for themselves, and some people think they are compassionate when they share another's pain, although they do not share his joy, but these are not the feelings of which I speak. The emotion I speak of isn't self-serving, nor does anyone who is compassionate ever feel better when someone they care about feels worse.

Real compassion is a strength born of a shared weakness, a recognition of a common humanity, a way of healing the wounds of separation by making connections, and it contains an acceptance of the fact that even in their deepest being, everyone is helpless and would welcome love from us.

Compassion passed through one person to another gives both the courage to live, and love pinched off and aborted hurts the one who lacks its courage as much as it injures the one who receives it not. And while it is often frightening to be like the bird that Victor Hugo described—"that pausing in her flight awhile on the boughs too slight, feels them give way beneath her and then sings knowing she has wings"—we have wings, nevertheless. And we have them most when we understand that love is capable of uniting human beings because it joins them by what is deepest in themselves.

Where does one find the courage to live with love's uncertainty? To stop running away from yourself, from life, and from your own vulnerability. And how does one finally come to understand that it is we ourselves who are the fountain and the feast, "the conveyer of divine sparks," as Martin Buber once said. And no one but we ourselves can warm our frozen heart.

I only know that while I fail where you fail and seek what you would find, I know as well that love is a burden if you can not give it, a pain if you can not feel it, and those who blunder into peace are those who learn to make a free gift of it, asking nothing back.

Where is he among us who dares speak of love, who dares speak of giving, of compassion, of that arc of feeling that flung out into the world can be followed back into one's self?

And does it really grow through fission and multiply with use, and disappear and dry up when one spends it not? And is it true that all those who husband and hoard and save their compassion only for themselves find themselves without it when they need it most?

I know the answer to this and so, of course, do you. But what I cannot answer and wish you would tell to me is why, if we know that compassion is an energy force which flows between all the world's creatures, do we guard it so. And why, if the problem is not getting it but releasing it, do we dam the flow?

The world is dying for lack of compassion. It is the food of life, so everyone must give what they can.

Whatever the question is, love is the answer, yet somehow there is never enough. But there could be as much as we need and then some. You just have to give yourself.

Some say love, it is a river that drowns the tender reeds,
Some say love, it is a razor, that leaves the soul to bleed,
Some say love, it is a hunger, an endless aching need,
I say love, it is a flower, but you must plant the seed.

—"The Rose"

*Part Four*

# 10

## *Love is more thicker than forget more thinner than recall*

I was curled up around a fire with a small group of friends one night, talking about life and what seemed to be important, and the conversation turned for a time to things one could not forgive. "There is one thing I can never forgive my mother for," a woman said, "and that is for continually telling me that having me had ruined her body and that she wished she'd never had a child at all."

"You think that was bad," another put in. "When my sister was killed, my father actually said right out it would have been better if it had been me, and I'll never be able to forgive him that. Never! Ever!"

"My father used to punish me," another woman added, "whenever he considered me to be deficient by phoning an imaginary little girl named Linda, who he claimed was perfect. And he'd croon to her on the phone about all the places he would take her and all the toys he'd buy for her, things he never did for me. And I can never forgive him that. And even now, long after, when he is in his late sixties and I am old enough to know better, whenever he comes to the house and visits with my children and I see him there sitting on the floor playing with them so nicely, I steel my heart against him. And a voice deep inside of me whispers, 'Don't forget Linda.' "

"Hearts will never be practical until they can be made unbreakable," the Wizard of Oz told the Tinman. And he was certainly right, because when we cannot forgive others, we break the bridge over which we must cross to find ourselves. As Martin Buber said, "He who passes sentence on a man has passed it on himself."


I am not speaking now of things one lets go of in time, of events that when you look back on them you wonder what made you consider them so upsetting when once you did. I am thinking more of the things that make us what we are, and what we might wish we weren't—the parent who wasn't really there, the sibling who was twice as fair, the lover who wasn't entirely true. And I am thinking of the things that we cannot change, or make them go away, because they aren't something else, or outside of us, but are our very selves, like the raindrops on a window that have joined up to become one. And so, when we hate those who laid the bruises on our soul, we hate in fact ourselves.

I knew a girl once who'd been the younger of two sisters, the older being more beautiful and a prodigy as well. And the mother spent herself on the older sister, leaving the younger one to grow up as she would. The younger sister learned to catch crumbs from the older one's table and to tap-dance to get the attention that she sought, and like the other family members, she paid homage to her older sister daily. But an enormous rage built up inside of her, and she couldn't control it; it swept her along in its wake.

I met her when she was already a woman, and one who knew all the tricks. She was a past master at manipulating others to get them to do as she wished. She had a husband she'd chosen for his malleability, and children she directed more than was good, and several careers begun and abandoned, but nothing of what she would. And still she curtsied to her sister, the anger growing harder to contain, and the distance between them in her mother's eyes growing greater as each decade and opportunity slipped away. Then finally, her sister grew ill, and she went to see her in her final days. And the sister spoke of how hard it had been for her to be the favorite, and to have to sing for her supper every day, and how much she resented her mother for making her earn her love with another accomplishment every year instead of just giving it unconditionally and loving her as she was. And the younger sister recognized that her sister wasn't the one who did it to her, but was a victim like herself, and that they both were done in by the same situation. And even her mother was to be pitied when you gave it thought, because she felt her own value derived from her children's accomplishments and did not feel valuable on her own.

U ntil one forgives, life is governed by an endless cycle of resentments and retaliations, and we spend our days scratching at the scabs on the wounds that we sustained long ago instead of letting them dry up and disappear.

There is no way to hate another that does not cost the hater, no way to remain unforgiving without maiming yourself, because undissolved anger stutters through the body of the person who can't forgive, short circuiting it and overloading it, and hatred makes gray days of ones that have sun.

"Hating people is like burning down your own house to get rid of a rat," Harry Emerson Fosdick said a long time ago, and it can't be put better today because the person who harbors a hatred for another immolates himself in his own fire.

There is a Zen story of two monks who come to a muddy road, and just as they are about to cross, a beautiful girl in a silk kimono and a long sash comes to cross as well. Seeing her distress at the condition of the road, one of the monks sweeps her up in his arms and carries her across. The other monk is astonished but says nothing. Finally, at night when they have arrived at the place of prayer, he speaks his mind. "Monks must have nothing to do with women," he tells his fellow monk. "It is very dangerous. You must stay away from them, and you must surely never touch them."

"Are you still carrying that maiden?" the first monk asks, astonished. "I put her down at the other side of the road, but you have carried her all this way."

I think some people cling to anger because to have been wronged makes them feel right. And they recite the horrors done to them as if they were saying a prayer inviting the gods to give them points for each wrong that they've endured. So important is it to them to confirm their rightness, that they dust off their hurts as often as they can and polish them until they gleam—feeling somehow that by so doing they have earned their keep. And they puff themselves up with their moral indignation like a child clings to a teddy bear for protection in the dark of the night.

It's as if they feel that if there is a bad guy, there must also be a good guy, and the worse the other guy is the better that makes them. And like the person who needs a triumph a day to keep his angst about his own powerlessness away, the person who believes in good guys and bad guys always needs a bad guy to affirm himself.

But the trouble with holding on to hurts, instead of letting them go, is that you continue to make decisions based on what hasn't been for a long time, and you live in that long ago, affixing fault and blame.

Some people do things to punish their mother, or to show him or her a thing or two, and some people do things to revenge themselves on another whoever that other might be. But as long as their actions don't come from positive feelings, but come instead from old angers, their defenses and self-doubts will multiply—and so, alas, will their inconsolable longings, their willful delusions, their repeat performances, and their doomed quests.

And they will spend their lives running hard, making decisions today and tomorrow that have to do with childhood furies and accidents of love, and never living in the present or becoming acquainted with what's now. Because when you don't learn from the past, you are doomed to repeat it, and until you forgive, you continue to impale yourself on your pain.

There was a boy once who was raised by his father after his parents divorced, and while he loved his father very much, he came to hate him too. His father was a harsh man on occasion, and the boy never somehow felt he measured up to his father's expectations. "If I didn't make the football team, he'd point out it was because I had my mother's coordination, and if I flunked math, he'd tell me my mother couldn't balance her chequebook. I guess in time I came to expect his putdowns, but the constant reference to my mother's flaws made me feel as if I was made out of ersatz goods, as if there was no way I could ever amount to anything, and I think I finally stopped trying.

"I must have remained in that state of thinking myself some kind of second-rate character, until I was almost a man, and then, by chance, I came to know my mother better and to realize that she had many fine qualities, several of which I recognized were also in myself. And then I really began to hate my father and to feel an enormous anger at him for all those years in which he kept me down by reciting all her bad qualities, for emphasizing her lack of sports ability when he could have as easily told me about her charm, and I hated him for a long time after that. I guess I hated him right up till I lost my first big love. And then I came to understand that he'd only told me of the bad things about my mother because he couldn't bear to remember the good ones, and that his constantly going on about her failures was a way of keeping his good memories at bay, a way of keeping his loss from overwhelming him when he saw her smiling at him from my eyes. And it wasn't until I had some compassion for him that I started to feel better about myself."

When you forgive, you take your enemy's power over you away, you defang them and change the atmosphere between you from highly charged to neutral, and sometimes even to rosy hued. And people, who had the power to control you just by being, can no longer command your emotions, or suck you into the vortex with a word. They cease to be the eye of your storm, and once you forgive them, they become people like any other, human and flawed and misguided on occasion, and hence rather like the rest of us.

Some say those who forgive are weak sisters, but I say that they are strong, because it takes a generous spirit to understand that people do not always hurt us because they choose to, but more because they couldn't help it or because we were in their way. And it takes a heart with lots of pluck to say when all is done, it didn't feel good when it happened, but I'd be a fool to let it do me any more harm than it already did.

No man knows the evil he does, and even if he should, the only thing to do when you feel hard-done-by is to act differently yourself. Because, it is when you forgive others that the gods forgive you, and you slip off the hook of your pain.

A broken heart can and must be mended, and it can be if we stop the chain. Because to look after your heart, you must use it, and to banish the ghosts that haunt you, you must smile them away.

There is a story by a famous Arab writer, Ali Yezzid Izz-Edin Ibn Salin Malba Tahan, about two friends who were traveling along one of the roads that wind among the dark and gloomy mountains of Persia, each of them accompanied by servants and caravans. At some point one of them lost his footing and fell into a whirling, foaming river, and the other, without hesitation, leaped in and saved him from drowning. The friend who almost drowned in the rapids called his most skilled slaves and ordered them to carve these words on a nearby black boulder. "Wanderer! In this place Nagib heroically saved the life of his friend Mussa."

After this had been done, the two friends continued on their journey, and after many months went by they came again to that very spot where the one had saved the other's life. They sat for a while and talked and then suddenly on some trifling matter they began to quarrel. Finally, in a fit of anger the one who had almost drowned was struck in the face by his friend, the one who had only last year saved him from the whirling river.

The one who was struck got up and, picking up his stick, wrote these words on the white sand near the black boulder. "Wanderer! In this place Nagib, in a trivial argument, broke the heart of his friend Mussa."

When one of Mussa's men inquired why he would record his friend's heroism in stone but his cruelty only in the sand, the wounded friend replied, "I shall cherish the memory of Nagib's brave assistance in my heart forever. But the grave injury he just gave me I hope will fade from my memory even before the words fade from the sand."

# 11

## *The brightest star in the darkest night*

The first night he took her out, he suggested they have a fling. "No thanks," she said without hesitating, "I am already flung out." He was somewhat taken aback, but tried again the next night. "You aren't offering me anything I need," she told him.

"I thought," he said, "a girl with your sophistication would be happy to have a relationship with no commitments."

"A girl of my sophistication," she answered with a smile, "knows that no commitments means there is no relationship."

"You understand what I mean?" he said, sounding annoyed.

"I think I do," she told him, "but explain it to me. When you offer me a fling, do you mean 'I am not taking this seriously and neither should you,' or do you mean 'I will give this my best shot for two or three weeks, but I don't want to be held responsible if it doesn't work.' "

He looked a bit sheepish. "I guess what I mean is I don't want a wake when it ends," he told her.

"We have just met and you are already checking the exits," she pointed out. "You are already thinking demise, having never thought delight."

Cynicism is a form of cowardice, a failure of courage to hope. So a lot of people ask others to let them out the side door of their lives, having never come in the front. And they sing a chorus of eat, drink, and be merry for tomorrow we die, while hedonism and pessimism play the accompanying tune.

There is a very strong connection between fear and hope and vulnerability, and when there is no hope there isn't any fear. So, for many, it is easier not to hope than to live with the vulnerability of expecting, to live with the fear of a hope one might not attain.

To hope is to set yourself up for a possible loss, so many people deny their hopes and by so doing detach themselves from what they want, not recognizing that hope is a forward scout on the path of time, and without it there is no tomorrow, there is not even much to be said for today.

To live without hope is to settle for grays, to say, "not me, not again, count me out." It is like being neutered, an existence, not a life, and one in which one neither soars nor swoops. In fact, to banish hope is a form of suicide, a kind of living death, yet many people choose it, believing that they protect themselves from risk.

There was a doctor once who was in love with a beautiful girl who had been a student of his. He was going to a foreign country to do some postgraduate work, and before he left, he asked her to marry him. And she, loving him but wanting time to realize some of her own dreams, asked for a year to think the matter over. She promised she would give him her answer before Christmas of the next year. He was disappointed when she did not say yes immediately, but he agreed to her terms, and then went away promising to write. And then one day she received a letter telling her he'd decided he could not live any longer with hope hanging like the sword of Damocles over his head, and so he'd married someone else.

There are so many stories about people who push love away because they fear to hope, people who foreclose on themselves for lack of trust. There are those who settle for second best, and the ones who love someone but tell them not, and those who hate someone because they failed to love someone else, and the ones who bring their relationship to convulsion when it looks like it has a chance because starting to hope again frightens them too much.

"Something we were witholding made us weak until we found it was ourselves," Robert Frost wrote. And, of course, the degree to which we are comfortable with our own needs is the degree to which we are comfortable with someone else's. So those who are the most in need usually deny their needs the most, and they run from those who offer love and from those who need them, because it is less painful to remain in the narrow room of self than it would be to open themselves up to hope.

It's the brave man who can live with hope and the fear that always travels close behind. And as far back as the ancient Greeks, it has been understood that where one goes, always comes the other. Pandora, they said, slipped the lid from a box, and all manner of plagues were loosed upon the world before she managed to jam the lid back on again. When she righted her mistake, hope and forboding only were left inside, and (so say the ancient Greeks) that is why, to this very day, man must fear whenever he hopes, but if he doesn't hope, all he has is fear.

You can play the same role all your life, if you want to, simply by not hoping. If you don't accept love when it is offered, don't ask for love when you need it, don't give love when you feel it. There will never be the pain of fears remembered or the danger of dreams rekindled, and you will never have to sacrifice what you are for what you could become.

And there are those who would rather deny their needs than risk a rejection, and those who are so afraid of being duped that they dupe themselves—as if they are saying deep down where no one but they can hear, "I could be an even greater fool and start to hope again." So they apply another poultice to their wounds instead and expose them to the air. And they collect a little more negative evidence and settle in for winter.

Perhaps despair is simply a hope that dies without being born and so turns against the one who would not let it grow and consumes him. And all those misconnections, all those warriors, crusaders, and zealous pilgrims on the road may simply be cowards who feared to hope, who skated on the possibility of their dreams and then turned tail and ran. And it could even be as well that those of us who never found what we dreamed of, may have found it a thousand times, but seeing only the thing we feared, chose to stay among the dispossessed.

There is a Sufi story I like about a beggar who approached a Mullah as he emerged from the mosque after prayers, and asked him for alms. "Are you extravagant?" the Mullah demanded of the beggar. The beggar answered yes. "Do you like sitting around drinking and smoking?" The beggar replied yes again. "I suppose you like to go to the baths every day?" The answer again was yes. "And maybe even amuse yourself by drinking with your friends?"

The beggar hung his head and said, "Yes, I like all these things."

"Tut, tut," answered the Mullah, and gave him a gold piece.

Another beggar nearby solicited the Mullah and was asked the same questions to which he replied, "No, no, no, I want only to live meagerly and pray!" The Mullah gave him a small copper coin.

"But why," wailed the beggar, "do you give me, an economical man, a penny when you give that extravagant fellow a gold sovereign?"

"Ah," replied the Mullah, "because his needs are greater than yours, I must give him more."

When you say, "This is what I need," you are halfway there to making your wish a reality. And as long as you say, "I don't really care," you never get what you care about. You get what you expect, which is to say to go on being disappointed.

"Whatever you can do, or dream you can do, begin it. Boldness has genius, power, and magic in it," Goethe wrote, and he was right. Our strength is in our dreams, and those who do not dare to dream damn themselves.

If you think of capital as time and health and companions to forge the river with, most of us have been issued with enough currency to purchase the good life, and there is no reason to opt for ashes in the mouth, no reason to be stuck in denial or grief unless you choose to be. You can change your karma—you've just to relate yourself with love to the world and accept the fact that we are never given a wish without the power to make that wish come true.

I know these are not times when one hopes easily or when one hopes without understanding one swims against the tide. And I am not recommending a disassociation from reality. Just an acceptance of the fact that each of us is the last frontier. There is a lack of generosity afoot today, an emotional frigidity, a "let me have it in writing" attitude that has trapped too many in self-pity and self-punishment, and if we want a better world there is nowhere to start but with ourselves.

Many years ago when I was newly separated and feeling very confused and lost, I went to see a bachelor friend who seemed to me to have mastered the art of living much better than anyone else I knew. He was eating his dinner and reading his paper when I came in, and as I talked about all the things bothering me, he went on eating and reading only nodding from time to time in my direction. Then when I had finally run out of words, he licked off his fork and, using it as a knife, excised from the newspaper a small square of paper and handed it to me. On it was printed "Make new friends." And I remember staring at that square of paper, wondering if he was mocking me, feeling what he expected of me was too tough, not knowing where to start, and wanting only to recite my woes again. But today I realize his advice was sound, that the answer always lies in hoping in the direction of your needs, and hoping in an active rather than a passive sense, which is to say not expecting the gods to read your mind but giving them a gentle assist. And if that means running the risk of disappointment, so be it. All of life is a risk, and if you choose life, you choose risk. "Not a victory is gained, not a deed of faithfulness or courage done," said William James, "except upon a maybe. And it is only by risking our persons from one hour to another that we live at all."

You can tell a lot about what a man lacks by watching what he is cynical about, and many of us are cynical about love. Enough in fact to make an epidemic. And it is possible to destroy yourself with disillusion without recognizing that it is you who holds the gun.

We can't will love, but we can will ourselves to be open to chance. We can will ourselves to choose life, just as we can will ourselves to shut off at some submerged, inarticulate place where we listen to ourselves even when we don't know what we've said.

And it is important to understand that not to say yes is to say no and that the road not taken sometimes affects our lives more than the path we choose, just as a meanness of spirit can choke the life from the person who denies himself and do more damage than anything done by someone else.

"To cheat oneself out of love is the most terrible deception; it is an eternal loss for which there is no reparation either in time or eternity," Kierkegaard said, and, of course, he was right.

A heart frozen against pain also stifles joy. And if every time hope flickers up like fever a small spasm of memory turns us sordid with self and we abdicate, we have canceled our own cheque, scratched ourselves before the race. And allowed the vain struggle to freeze out the pain, to freeze out meaning and pleasure as well.

T he Irish from the district of Carlingford tell this legend about healing yourself.

Close to the ancient cemetery of Kilbroney, under a great ash tree, there is a spring called "Saint Brigid's Well," held sacred by the people of the locality as similar springs are venerated in every parish in the country, and in every country in the world, for the curing mineral qualities they possess.

The well was sought by people who resorted to the well mirror when they wished to scan the future or longed to gaze backward in its waters of memory. And to those who drank of its waters before sunrise of the spring festival, it was believed to give great knowledge and was called The Well of Wisdom and All-Healing.

The well ran dry for some many centuries after it had been desecrated, but then in Christian times, when the virgin Saint Bronach was killed on the site by a band of Scandinavian pirates, a new spring burst out of the ground on the fatal spot.

After that, every year on the anniversary of Saint Bronach's martyrdom, the waters would boil up, overflowing the meadows. And pilgrims would come from all parts of the province to bathe their eyes or other afflicted parts in this well of all-healing, where the well water was reputed to possess the virtue of making people, so wishing, young and beautiful if they bathed their faces in the well at midnight on the eve of Bronach's Feast.

It happened once that on the evening before the Virgin Martyr's Festival there was a great feasting in the halls of Castle Rory to celebrate a victorious campaign of Chief Rory MacGuinness. At this evening's banquet there was present the daughter of one of the "Urighs" named Blamha. She had been born blind and spent her early years in total darkness. But two years before this, she had miraculously received the gift of sight by going to the holy well at midnight on the feast eve and bathing her eyes in the waters, and they were opened instantly.

But the gift of sight served to make her aware of a fact she was ignorant of before. She was ugly, and now she understood why the young Rory MacGuinness could not bear to look on her, even though she had given her love to him secretly when she was blind.

Blamha felt her affliction most keenly this night, and she was bemoaning her fate when suddenly she remembered that this was the eve of Saint Bronach's Feast—tonight the waters were potent to make her beautiful.

At once she left the gay halls of Castle Rory resolving to implore the good saint of the well to make her beautiful this night or, failing that, to strike her blind again. She knelt on her knees in front of the well and was preparing to bathe her face when she saw a bright tablet over the well on which was written in fiery letters this message:

"It is not necessary to bathe your face in the sacred spring to gain beautiful features. Without this water's aid, you can be lovely, for beauty is the soul shining from the eyes. You must think beauty and admire it in everything—landscape, face, and flower—and control all emotions of envy, jealousy, discontent, and revenge, for ugly thoughts make the countenance ugly. Mould your body by your mind and gain the good qualities. Do this and all hearts will love you."

And as Blamha read, the words died out, and the tablet faded before her eyes.

She rose from her knees without bathing her face. Her eyes sparkled, and her face shone with the anticipated pleasure of life heretofore denied her. Already she had changed. The demon of ugliness had departed, and the spirit of beauty had come to stay with her. She lived life as advised and got more beautiful all the time as promised, and numerous were the suitors for her hand, but the young chief of Castle Rory remained her choice, and soon he made her his bride.

To many, hope is an illusion, a trap, a lollipop proferred in lieu of what they want, so they refuse to hope, refuse to invest themselves in anything that isn't a sure thing. To them, hope is to reality what the mirage is to the oasis, just a trick your psyche plays on you and a sure sign that you are losing your grip.

And others think of hope as a waiting game, a gift dependent on the whims of others not themselves, and they spend their days plea bargaining with the gods, and pray for luck as if their life were a ripple to someone else's thrown stone.

But I think of hope as a way of healing, a miracle cure—you've just to believe in it for it to work. And I think of hope as the stroke of grace that transcends all the pain, a kind of aurora borealis of the soul without which our hearts could never feast, or we become the selves we were meant to be.

"Hope is a state of pregnancy, a species of happiness in itself," Samuel Johnson said, "and perhaps the chief happiness which this world affords." And when you have hope, anything is possible—things that would otherwise never be—because you give birth to them yourself.

"Hope is the thing with feathers," Emily Dickenson wrote, "That perches in the soul. And sings the tune without the words / And never stops at all."

# 12

## *Don't be alone too long*

There was a couple once who seemed perfect for each other. They even looked like they were made for each other. Both of them were tall with tawny coloring. A union made in heaven others said, and for some time it was.

They furnished an apartment, made some friends, had a baby, and then he began to wander. First, he just seemed distracted when she tried to talk to him. She worried that she was getting boring. Then he began to stay late at the office. She alternately worried that he was working too hard and having an affair. "There is no reason for you and me to limit our lives just to each other," he told her one evening when she screwed up her courage enough to ask him.

"I don't want anyone but you," she told him, tears already starting in her eyes. "That's because you don't know anyone else," he assured her. "You should get out more."

After that he didn't come home some nights, and he didn't explain. She stood it as long as she could, and then she took the baby and went home to her mother. "You are being silly," he told her as she packed. "I wish you weren't so childish. Everyone has affairs. There is no reason to break up a marriage."

For six months she cried, and then she went back to University. She got up every morning at six A.M. and fed and dressed the baby and took him to a day care center, and then she went to school. Her mother picked the baby up at night and gave him supper and looked after him in the evening while she stayed late at the library. It wasn't easy and it wasn't fun, but there wasn't anything else she could do. Besides, it kept her too busy to think.

One weekend each month he stopped in to see the baby. She noticed he was looking strung out in recent visits, but she didn't say anything. One Sunday he asked her if she would like to have a talk. "We could have dinner or lunch if you would like." She nodded numbly, not knowing why. "I want you back," he told her as they neared dessert. "I have learned something very important in the last two years. I have learned that there is nobody better out there. I always felt there might be, and I had to find out for myself."

"I always felt there might be somebody better out

there too," she told him, feeling sure of herself for the first time in a long while, "but I stayed with you anyway. That's why my staying had meaning. It doesn't mean anything to me that you want me back now that you have found out there isn't anyone better. You are talking about opportunism. I am talking about love."

The fifties were a time of commitment. And personal growth and freedom were sacrificed for it. And then the sixties came along, and the banner of freedom was held on high but commitment somehow got lost along the way. There was something about the "free to be me" message of the sixties that was a siren's song, and a lot of people rushed to get into the swim, and many of them dived in before anyone told them where the shallow water was, and a lot of them were never the same again.

There was a time when we said, "No one is perfect," and now we say, "No one is perfect enough," while we wait for the flawless one just off the horizon, the one we've yet to meet. And we think that loving everyone is the same as loving in particular, and so we are alone.

We live in a world that doesn't reflect spiritual values, so a lot of people have lost their moral compasses, and they wander through life confused. To them, self-fulfillment is an inner journey, and others are only guides and hotelkeepers along the way. So personal freedom is what's valued most highly, and commitment is seen as a threat to it, something to be feared and avoided, not something to welcome and embrace.

We live at a time when the idea of commitment seems to carry a negative weight, and people think you have to give up something if you commit instead of feeling that commitment means making fast a dream. So people don't commit these days, they make deals instead, agreeing only, "I'll do this for you if you'll do this for me." And they trade in promissory notes redeemable without penalty, and at any time.

A lack of commitment is the disease of our generation, and a lot of people wish they felt more committed, wish they had something to commit to, wish they felt a bit more engagé, without realizing you can't be committed to anything if you aren't committed to yourself.

Commitment isn't a station you arrive at; it's a by-product of something else, and I think the something else is believing that what you do matters and acting on that belief. And when you feel yourself to be empty, when you feel yourself somehow not to count, you keep feeling that someone else or something else might do it, might save you from yourself. So your goal becomes keeping your options open, and commitment is seen as a threat to what might be, not as a statement of what you are—which is what it really is.

"I am the sum of my commitments," Martin Buber said, "or, in other words, I am what I chose to stand up and be counted for, and those choices define me." Which means, of course, that all those people who don't commit, all those people who are acting like they are not really on this trip, and all those people who have put themselves on hold, they are cheating themselves, and in seeking to have wings, they've forgotten that they need roots as well.

I was at a party once when a woman began to talk with some distress about her marriage of eighteen years, which had begun to flounder. It had been a good marriage for many years, fed by the silent springs of much money and the advantages that such can buy. There were the twice-annual trips to Paris on business, designer clothes new each season, exotic vacations for the whole family every quarter, and dinner parties in their penthouse apartment, the table wreathed with celebrities and stars.

Everything had begun to go wrong when the husband sold his business for a large sum of money and began to cast about for something to do with his life. Soon he'd begun to doubt himself and, in doubting himself, to doubt his marriage. These nights, instead of dining with his wife and children and their guests, he went roller-skating with strangers she did not know. There was the suggestion of drugs and infidelity. He would not answer her questions. He had bought a yacht and was talking of sailing around the world.

The wife was in despair about the drugs and other women. He'd begun to spend money in an irresponsible way. Hangers-on had appeared from every quarter to help him enjoy the fruits of his labor. Her brother had warned her to take him to court before he ran through his whole fortune and left her and the kids impoverished. Her mother was furious about the way he was behaving, and was urging a divorce as well, telling her she was still young and could get another husband easily.

The others at the party agreed. "You don't have to put up with this," they said.

And then she turned to me. "What do you think?" she asked.

I hesitated for a moment, knowing my view ran counter to the rest. "Well," I said, "you got married for better or for worse, and you have undoubtedly had better, but if your husband came down with diabetes or a heart condition, you wouldn't be talking divorce, and this is a disease of sorts as well, so I think you should stay and show you care."

Who is there amongst us who dares to speak of loyalty or love, and, of course, I know that one person's commitment is another's fling, but I should just like to say this: that I hold to be the highest task of a bond between two people that each should stand guard over the vulnerability of the other. And that we all must understand that what is lacking in our world is trust, and if what we want is to be able to trust, then we must be trustworthy, because those who betray are betrayed, and those who doubt are doubted, and the buck always stops with us.

We have all been living off our moral capital for a long time, and none of us can say who should be the accusers and who the accused, but sometimes the pearl in the head of the toad is hard to see until one has to look for it, and if a commitment ceases to be a commitment if we don't get our terms, and if we cease to care when there are no guarantees, it does not appear at all.

There is no more purpose in this world than you put in to it, so it is up to each one of us. I once heard a minister say, "If you want to grow for today, grow vegetables. If you want to grow for tomorrow, grow trees. But if you want to grow for the future, grow families," and his point was well made. There is the short term and the long term, and one must keep them both in sight. And it is also true that many of us who thought we married the wrong mate learn finally and too late that it wasn't so much that he was the wrong person but that we weren't the right person ourselves that finally caused the break.

I don't know where we got the idea that it is an either/or situation, that it's freedom or commitment, personal growth or responsibility, and that if we choose commitment it will be our loss and not our gain. Because one grows in commitment, one doesn't diminish—in fact, it is the only way to grow. And if you commit to nothing but yourself, you pour yourself into the thirsty distance, having nothing to show for it but the cancers on your soul. And you learn too late, as many people have, that man is a ladder, and each rung that takes us higher is a responsibility accepted gratefully, and that there is no personal growth without responsibility, and no such thing as freedom without commitment, nor can there ever be.

Once when Care was crossing a river, an ancient fable of Hyginus tells us, she saw some clay, and she thoughtfully took up a piece and began to shape it. While she was meditating on what she had made, Jupiter came by. Care asked him to give it spirit, and this he gladly granted. But when she wanted her name to be bestowed upon it, he forbade this, and demanded that it be given his name instead. While Care and Jupiter were disputing, Earth arose and desired that her own name be conferred on the creature, since she had furnished it with part of her body. They asked Saturn to be their arbiter, and he made the following decision, which seemed a just one: "Since you, Jupiter, have given it spirit, you shall receive the spirit at its death; and since you, Earth, have given its body, you shall receive its body. But since Care first shaped this creature, she shall possess it as long as it lives."

Euripides said, "Man's life and care are twins and born one day." And one could safely say it is through caring that we live, and through what we care about that we grow into what we were meant to be. And those who do not care about anything but themselves, become nothing much at all, because it is through what we invest with ourselves that we grow rich in life. And through our connectedness to others that we connect with ourselves.

"There is only a single magic, a single power, a single salvation and a single happiness, and that is called loving," Herman Hesse wrote in a book of his essays called *My Beliefs*, and I would side with him on that. As there is no better way I know out of yourself, no better way to become yourself, no better way to save yourself than love.

> Ah love, let us be true
> To one another! For the world, which seems
> To lie before us like a land of dreams,
> So various, so beautiful, so new,
> Hath really neither joy, nor love, nor light,
> Nor certitude, nor peace, nor help for pain;
> And we are here as on a darkling plain
> Swept with confused alarms of struggle and flight,
> Where ignorant armies clash by night.
> —*Mathew Arnold*, "Dover Beach"

*About the Author*

Merle Shain lives and works in Toronto, Canada. She graduated from university with a degree in social work, practiced for several years, and more recently has worked as a magazine editor, a newspaper columnist, a feature writer, a critic, and a television host and interviewer. She has been married and has a son.